G.R.E.A.T.

is for a

DAY WITH MY GRANDPARENTS!

Written By: Jadedra Gilmore-Barber
Illustrated By: Elfaza Studio

Published by: EarKanDee LLC
For more information: earkandee.educate@gmail.com
ISBN: 979-8-9910746-4-3
www.earkandeeonline.com

EST 2024

Ear Kan Dee

listen design, discover

"If better is possible, good is not enough."
— Benjamin Franklin

To my son,
Always remember mommy's love for you is infinite.

Acknowledgements

To my husband,
Thank you for showing me daily the meaning of perseverance.

To my son,
You are so brave and joyful. You inspire me each day.

To my father and mother,
The wind beneath my wings.

To my brother,
The visionary.

To my family and friends,
The roots that keep me grounded.

My Lord and Savior,
Thank you God for your continued grace and guidance.

I love you all.

Table of Contents

Characters

Grandad

Grandma

King

Good Food!

Hi! My name is King, but my grandad nicknamed me Tank!

I always have a GREAT time spending the day with my grandparents. We always start the day with my favorite breakfast, chicken biscuits and a hashbrown casserole! Mmh mmh, GOOD!

Rock and Rest!

My grandparents love to dance! OUT-STAND-ING! I get so excited, I want to SHOUT! We play games, read books, and make funny faces, especially during diaper changes! At noon is nap time. My grandma says it is because I am young, and she doesn't want me to get restless. My grandad said naptime is what helped my grandmom stay bold and beautiful, even at her old age of 26!

BLE!

5

When I asked my mom about noon naps, she told me grandma just likes to watch soap operas. She asked me to promise not to tell that's where Uncle Vic's name came from! I will never understand why my grandma enjoys watching people play with soap while singing on stage. Isn't that how soap and operas work? Oh, well, "That's her business" as Ms. Tab says.

Eating Snacks!

SNACK TIME! Another great part of my day with my grandparents. My grandad makes me a cold bowl of watermelon. YUM, YUM, YUM! Sometimes I eat peaches too! Woo wee, they are GOOD!

<u>A</u> Walk Around!

After snack time, my grandma and grandad take me for a walk. Sometimes, my grandad sits me on his shoulders. WOW, I think I can touch the sky! My grandma laughs as my grandad shouts,

"Hey bird, don't you bother my grandson!"

_Time to Go!

I always get big hugs from my grandparents when the day ends. I wave bye and cannot wait for another GREAT day with my grandparents!

Comprehension Questions

1. What are King's favorite breakfast foods?
a. applesauce
b. peaches
c. chicken biscuits and hashbrown casserole

2. When does King take a nap?
a. in the morning
b. at noon
c. when he goes home

3. Using the table of contents, what pages would you find information about "Eating Snacks"?
a. 8-9
b. 10-11
c. 12-13

4. What does King always get when his day ends with his grandparents?
a. hugs
b. candy
c. toys

Sight Words

Primer

- but
- eat
- have
- to
- with
- they

- good
- are
- get
- so
- want
- at

- am
- what
- she
- came
- will
- on
- that

Pre-Primer

- my
- where
- is
- can
- me
- big
- I

- for
- a
- the
- with
- we
- and

- to
- play
- make
- funny
- it
- not

First Grade

- of
- when
- from
- just

- how
- her
- as
- after

- his
- think
- walk

Second Grade

- tell
- always
- because

- read
- why

- cold
- work

Third Grade

- never
- about

Writing Fun!

Personalize Your Book! Use the sight words to write about a day you enjoyed spending with your grandparents!

My Grandparents Photos!

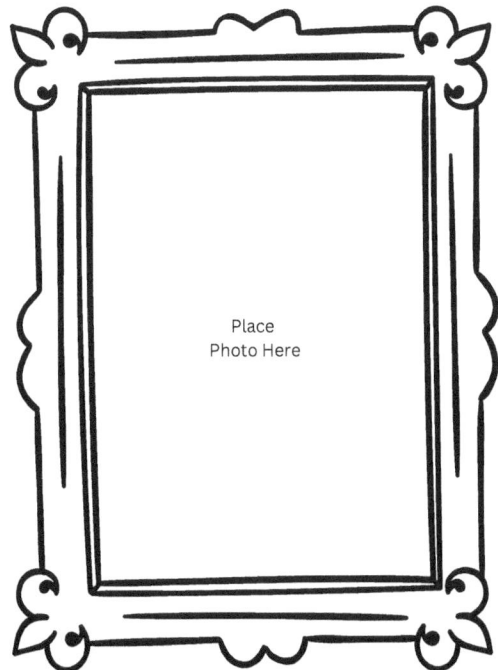

Place
Photo Here

Place
Photo Here

Biography

Dr. Jadedra Gilmore-Barber was born and raised in Fort Valley, Georgia. She has been an educator for over 14 years. Dr. Gilmore-Barber has held various roles during her years in the field of education. She has served as a teacher, academic coach, and administrator. She graduated from Georgia Southwestern State University with a bachelor's degree in Early Childhood Education, a master's degree in Curriculum and Instruction, and a specialist degree in Teacher Leadership. She graduated from Columbus State University with a specialist add-on in Educational Leadership, and a doctoral in Educational Leadership. Dr. Gilmore-Barber's philosophy of education is "Where better is possible, good is not enough!" She strives to motivate students to gain and maintain a love of learning.

www.ingramcontent.com/pod-product-compliance
Lightning Source LLC
Chambersburg PA
CBHW040231070426
42447CB00030B/149